Short Stack Editions | Volume 3

Strawberries
by Susan Spungen

Short Stack Editions

Publisher: Nick Fauchald
Creative Director: Rotem Raffe
Editor: Kaitlyn Goalen
Copy Editor: Abby Tannenbaum
Marketing Manager: Erin Fritch

Text and recipes copyright © 2013 Susan Spungen (SusanSpungen.com).
Design and illustrations copyright © 2013 Rotem Raffe.
All rights reserved to Short Stack Editions.
Distributed in the United States by Dovetail Press (dovetail.press).
No portion of this book may be used or reproduced in any manner
whatsoever without written permission of the publisher.

ISBN 978-0-9896017-2-6

Printed in Virginia
Fourth printing, July 2017

Table of Contents

From the Editors — 5
Introduction — 7

Salads, Starters & Savories

Cold Soba Salad — 12
Baby Greens Salad with Strawberries & Pickled Ramps — 14
Peanut Butter, Strawberry & Bacon Sandwich — 15
Strawberry Tartines with Ricotta & Basil Oil — 16

Preserves and Pickles

Strawberry Compound Butter — 17
Pickled Strawberries — 18
Strawberry Freezer Jam — 20

Condiments

Slow-Roasted Strawberries & Tomatoes — 22
Strawberry, Tomato & Avocado Salsa — 23

Tarts and Crisps

Strawberry Tart with Goat Cheese Filling — 24
Strawberry Tarte Tatin — 26
Strawberry, Apricot & Almond Tart — 28

Strawberry Hand Pies — 30
Gingered Strawberry-Rhubarb Crisp — 32

Frozen Desserts

Ice Pops with Hazelnut Chocolate — 34
Roasted Strawberry-Basil Frozen Yogurt — 35

Other Desserts

Lemony Cornmeal Strawberry Shortcakes — 36
Summer Berry Pudding — 38
Eton Mess — 40

Drinks

Strawberry Smoothie — 42
Pink Sangria — 43

Thank You! — 45
Colophon — 47

There are times when it seems silly to hold onto every single cookbook and food magazine we come across (the last time we moved, the number of boxes we needed to pack up our culinary library was like something out of *Hoarders*).

But the doubt never remains for long. Any time we think about what to make for lunch or how to use the strawberries we just scored at the market, our bookshelf becomes an indispensable chorus of old friends, their suggestions indexed by past experiences. When it comes to cooking wisdom and inspiration, digital bookmarks can't compare with dog-eared, sauce-stained pages.

It was in this spirit that we set out to create Short Stack Editions, the third of which you now hold in your hands. The author of this edition, Susan Spungen, is already a legend in many cooks' libraries, a familiar author of multiple books and countless magazine recipes. We can't imagine anyone better suited to feature in this new publication, which spotlights inspiring ingredients through the work of innovative, intelligent authors.

Short Stack is our argument in favor of the printed cookbook. It's our stab at combining everything we love about food into a petite package: reliable recipes, beloved ingredients, clever ideas, culinary talents, beautiful design and a real-life community of cooks.

Thank you for making space on your bookshelf; we're excited to earn our place.

—*The Editors*

Introduction

In my opinion, strawberries are the best of all berries. Neither blueberries nor raspberries offer as much in terms of flavor and versatility. And that divine smell! The perfume clings to my fingers even as I write this. I truly think strawberries are one of nature's greatest gifts.

The funny thing is, I didn't even like strawberries when I was a child. Like many kids, I didn't like foreign objects to interfere with my food and, to me, the seeds were an interference. I'm so glad I outgrew that idiosyncrasy a long time ago. Today, I can't get enough of them.

To me, there are two kinds of strawberries. The first is the large, dense variety from California that's available at the supermarket year-round. These strawberries have been bred to withstand long-distance shipping and look glossy and inviting in the fruit aisle for days on end, but those traits have been enhanced at the expense of flavor and texture (no offense, California). The second is the highly seasonal strawberries that you'll find at your farmers' market. It doesn't matter where you live: Whatever locally grown strawberries you can get your hands on are going to be eons better than those that are on sale at the supermarket.

However, supermarket strawberries—our only option for much of the year—can be put to good use. Flavor can be coaxed out of them, especially through cooking, and their firmness can actually work to your advantage in a salad. Don't bother trying to make jam out of them, though; save that activity until you've stockpiled enough of the juicy little red ones during their very short season.

When strawberry season begins here on the East Coast in late spring, I go into a bit of a frenzy. I buy too many to consume and, when my surplus threatens to spoil, I freeze them for smoothies, crisps and pies. (It's a great consolation to open my freezer and see great quantities of frozen berries when the fresh ones have already disappeared from the stands.)

The recipes in this little edition explore the possibilities of cooking with strawberries. Some are familiar, such as my take on strawberry shortcake (made with cornmeal biscuits and a satiny lemon cream) or the crowd-pleasing strawberry-rhubarb crisp (this time laced with three kinds of ginger).

I also wanted to upend expectations of how strawberries could be used: Why not put them in a cold soba noodle salad with charred shishito peppers and miso dressing? They add a pleasantly juicy note, a great contrast of flavor and an undeniable splash of beauty. Bakers, longtime champions of the strawberry, have plenty of fodder to work with here: This edition contains no fewer than four tarts, each completely different, from the very easy but irresistible hand pie to the more advanced strawberry tarte Tatin.

I hope you enjoy this array of recipes, and I sincerely hope you'll add some of them to your own strawberry repertoire.

—*Susan Spungen*

Recipes

Strawberry Yields Forever

Strawberry weights and volumes can vary considerably, especially when you compare farmers' market strawberries with the larger, heavier variety you'll find at the supermarket year-round. Most of the recipes in this book call for the volume measurement of the prepared (i.e., hulled and sliced, hulled and quartered, etc.) amount. To make shopping easier, I've created this handy chart to help you figure out how much you'll need to buy.

Large Strawberries

	whole		hulled		hulled and quartered/sliced
1 pound =	4 CUPS	=	3½ CUPS	=	3 CUPS
½ pound =	2 CUPS	=	1¾ CUPS	=	1½ CUPS
¼ pound =	1 CUP				

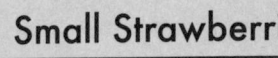

Small Strawberries

	whole		hulled		hulled and quartered/sliced
1 pound =	4 CUPS	=	3¾ CUPS	=	3½ CUPS
½ pound =	2 CUPS	=	SCANT 2 CUPS	=	1¾ CUPS
¼ pound =	1 CUP				
1 pint =	8 TO 12 OUNCES		=		2 TO 3 CUPS WHOLE
1 quart =	1 TO 1½ POUNDS		=		4 TO 6 CUPS WHOLE

Cold Soba Salad

To me, there is nothing more refreshing for a warm-weather meal than a cold noodle salad. Although adding strawberries to a salad like this may seem unusual—and it is—the combination really works. The juiciness of the berries adds a cool and sweet-tart contrast to the slight spiciness of the peppers and the salty miso dressing. The salad can marinate and improve for several hours or even a day or two, but the strawberries won't hold up well, so toss them in just before serving. This salad would go very well with anything off the grill, especially chicken, flank steak and pork tenderloin.

For the dressing:

¼ cup rice wine vinegar

1 tablespoon sugar

1 teaspoon salt

2 tablespoons white miso

1 hot red chile, finely minced, or more to taste

2 tablespoons dark sesame oil

serves 8

For the salad:

One 8.8-ounce package soba noodles

4 ounces shishito peppers (if they're not in season, substitute cubanelle or poblano peppers)

½ cucumber—peeled, seeded and thinly sliced on the bias into ¼-inch half moons

2 cups strawberries, hulled and halved (about ½ pound whole)

2 scallions, thinly sliced

¼ cup mint, roughly chopped

¼ cup cilantro, roughly chopped

Make the dressing: Stir the rice vinegar, sugar and salt together until the sugar and salt have dissolved. Add the miso, chile and sesame oil; whisk to combine. Set aside.

Cook the noodles according to package directions. Drain and rinse with cool water. Drain well. Toss the noodles with the dressing.

Grill the shishito peppers on a grill or grill pan or in a cast-iron skillet until they're blistered and softened, about 2 to 3 minutes a side. Let them cool, then slice on a bias and discard the seeds.

Top the dressed noodles with the grilled peppers, cucumbers, strawberries, scallions, mint and cilantro. Mix gently to combine and serve.

Baby Greens Salad with Strawberries & Pickled Ramps

For just a few moments in the spring, ramps and strawberries overlap at my local farmers' market in New York City. I quickly get to pickling the short-lived ramps so that I can use them in this recipe as long as possible. If ramps are hard to come by where you live, red onions are a fine stand-in. The best salads somehow make discordant ingredients sing together in harmony, and this one is no exception.

For the dressing:

1 tablespoon finely chopped shallot

2 teaspoons honey mustard

2 tablespoons fresh lemon juice

6 tablespoons extra-virgin olive oil

Salt and freshly ground pepper

For the salad:

8 cups mixed baby greens and/or arugula

2 cups strawberries, hulled and sliced crosswise (about ½ pound whole)

8 pickled ramps (recipe follows), sliced crosswise into rounds (about ½ cup)

¼ cup raw pistachios, coarsely chopped

3 ounces goat cheese, crumbled

Salt and freshly ground pepper

serves 4

In a bowl, add the dressing ingredients and whisk to combine. Divide the greens among four plates. Top each plate with a quarter of the strawberries, ramps, pistachios and goat cheese. Drizzle each plate with dressing, season to taste with salt and pepper and serve.

Pickled Ramps

1 cup white wine vinegar

1 cup apple cider vinegar

¼ cup sugar

1 tablespoon plus 1 teaspoon kosher salt

1 pound ramps, greens and roots trimmed, leaving just the bulb and stem

In a medium saucepan over medium heat, add the vinegars, sugar, kosher salt and 2½ cups of water and bring to a boil. Simmer until the sugar and salt have dissolved. Place the trimmed ramps in a nonreactive bowl and cover with the liquid. Allow the ramps to cool, then transfer them to a lidded jar and refrigerate for at least one day and up to one month.

Peanut Butter, Strawberry & Bacon Sandwich

I grew up eating peanut butter and bacon sandwiches, which seemed odd to some people until a few years ago, when every chef and food writer became fascinated with pairing bacon with all kinds of sweets. Maybe it was Elvis who started the trend, or maybe it was a thing in my native Philadelphia (I'll have to ask my mother). In any case, it is essential that the bacon be very crisp, the peanut butter smooth and creamy, and the bread soft. The bacon should be the only crunchy thing in the sandwich.

In a skillet, cook **2 slices of bacon** until very crisp. Drain on a paper towel. Spread **1 slice of white bread** with **creamy peanut butter** and top with the bacon. Spread **1 slice of white bread** with **crushed strawberries** or **Strawberry Freezer Jam** (page 20), press the 2 slices together and serve.

Strawberry Tartines with Ricotta & Basil Oil

Whether you call them tartines or crostini, these little toasts are an easy and beautiful way to enjoy strawberries. This recipe is especially good with tiny ruby red strawberries from your local farmers' market. For breakfast, switch out the basil and basil oil for honey and mint.

For the basil oil:
1½ cups basil leaves
½ cup extra-virgin olive oil

For the tartines:
1 baguette
1½ cups ricotta
2 cups strawberries, hulled and sliced lengthwise (about ½ pound whole)
1 teaspoon aged balsamic vinegar
Salt and freshly ground pepper
4 basil leaves, thinly sliced into ribbons, for garnish

serves 4

Make the basil oil: Bring a small saucepan of water to a boil. Blanch the basil for 10 seconds, then transfer immediately to a bowl of ice water. Squeeze the leaves dry, then transfer them to a blender and add the olive oil. Puree, then strain the oil through a fine-mesh sieve. (The oil can be refrigerated for up to 1 week.)

Make the tartines: Cut the baguette on a bias into 6-inch-long slices. Toast (about 12 minutes in a 375° oven) or grill until golden brown. Spread each slice with ricotta and top with a heaping spoonful of sliced strawberries. Drizzle with some of the vinegar and basil oil. Top with salt, pepper and some of the basil leaves and serve.

Strawberry Compound Butter

Compound butters are like an instant sauce: They can be made with anything and they melt into a delicious puddle when placed on top of a hot dish. The heat of the food releases the aromas and flavors of the ingredient—in this case, strawberries. Cooking the strawberries not only intensifies and concentrates their flavor, but it also lowers the moisture content so they blend smoothly with the butter. Use this butter on toast, pancakes and waffles.

- 1 cup strawberries, hulled (about 3 ounces whole)
- 1 tablespoon honey
- 1 stick (8 tablespoons) unsalted butter, at room temperature

In a food processor, combine the strawberries and honey and process until smooth. Transfer to a small saucepan and simmer over medium heat until reduced by half. Transfer to a bowl and refrigerate until cool, about 15 minutes.

Once the strawberry mixture has cooled, return it to the food processor with the butter and pulse until fully combined.

Place the strawberry butter in the center of a sheet of wax paper or parchment paper, then fold the bottom of the sheet of paper over the butter to align it with the top of the sheet. Hold on to the bottom piece of paper and, using one edge of a baking sheet, push against the butter until it forms a neat 6-inch log. Twist the paper ends and wrap the log in plastic wrap. Refrigerate until firm and slice into rounds as needed. The butter will keep for a week in the refrigerator or a month in the freezer.

Pickled Strawberries

Pickling is a great way to preserve this fragile fruit for just a little bit longer than the duration of the season. You can improvise with the ingredients—and the amount of sugar and salt—depending on how you want to use the pickled berries. If you plan to use them to top ice cream or even a shortcake (like the one on page 36), keep the vanilla bean and the listed amount of sugar. If you'd like a more savory result as a topping for salads, replace the vanilla bean with a teaspoon of whole coriander seeds and cut the sugar to 1 tablespoon. You could also use rosemary or thyme instead of mint. Either way, the picked berries are supereasy, look pretty in a jar and will keep for a couple of weeks in the fridge. The leftover pickling liquid (aka "shrub") makes a tasty addition to a soda or a cocktail.

½ cup regular rice wine vinegar (not seasoned)

3 tablespoons sugar

½ teaspoon kosher salt

1 teaspoon black peppercorns

½ vanilla bean, split lengthwise

2 sprigs mint

2¼ cups strawberries, hulled (about ½ pound whole)

Two 8-ounce canning jars or one 16-ounce canning jar, sanitized and completely dry

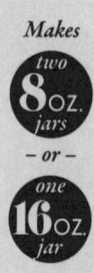

Makes two 8 oz. jars – *or* – one 16 oz. jar

In a medium saucepan, bring the vinegar, sugar, salt, peppercorns, vanilla bean and ½ cup of water to a boil. Simmer until the sugar and salt have dissolved. Let cool until lukewarm.

Meanwhile, place 1 sprig of mint into each 8-ounce canning jar. Cut a shallow X into the hulled end of each strawberry and divide between the jars. (If you're using one larger jar, combine the mint and strawberries.)

Once the vinegar mixture has cooled slightly, pour it into the jar(s) over the strawberries and mint. Seal and refrigerate overnight. The pickled strawberries will keep for 1 to 2 weeks in the refrigerator.

Strawberry Freezer Jam

When strawberries are at their peak, I get the urge to preserve. I am not an expert, though, and don't have the equipment or inclination to practice traditional canning. Freezer jam promised to be an appealing middle ground, but I had trouble finding a reliable formula. Fortunately, I was rescued by a recipe from Afton Hall of Cheyenne, Wyo., the mother of my assistant Pearl Jones. It works perfectly, producing a looser-than-normal jam that can also be used as a sauce to serve over ice cream or pancakes.

6 heaping cups whole strawberries, hulled and quartered, about 1¾ pounds

3 cups sugar, divided

One 1.75-ounce box Sure-Jell Fruit Pectin for Less or No Sugar Needed Recipes

makes 3 to 6 jars

In a large bowl, lightly crush the strawberries with the back of a wooden spoon. Place a fine-mesh sieve over another bowl and strain the strawberries. Transfer 4 cups of the crushed strawberries to a medium bowl and add 2 cups of the sugar. Let sit for 30 minutes. Add the remaining crushed strawberries to the bowl with the reserved juice. Crush a bit more (you should have approximately 1 cup of the strawberry mixture), then set aside.

In a medium pot, combine the remaining cup of sugar and the pectin. Add the strawberry-juice mixture to the pot and bring to a boil over medium-high heat, stirring constantly. Boil for 1 minute while stirring, then remove from the heat. Stir in the reserved strawberry-sugar mixture and stir for 1 minute more, until well blended and the sugar has dissolved.

Divide the jam among six 8-ounce jars or three 16-ounce jars, leaving ½ inch of space between the jam and the lip of the jar. Seal and let the jam sit at room temperature for 24 hours. The jam can also be stored in resealable plastic bags. Store in the refrigerator for up to 3 weeks or in the freezer for up to a year.

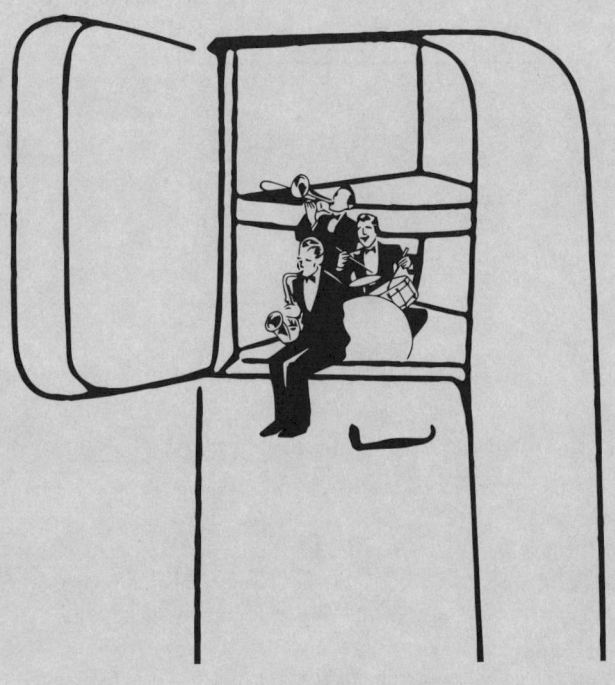

Slow-Roasted Strawberries & Tomatoes

I've noticed that the acidity levels of strawberries and tomatoes are not so very different, nor is the moisture content. As a result, I've taken to slow-roasting the two together, which creates a tart-sweet condiment that makes a nice addition to a cheese plate or salad, a topping for crostini or a bright surprise served alongside roasted or grilled pork or chicken.

3½ cups strawberries, hulled and halved, quartered if large (13 ounces)

2½ cups grape tomatoes, halved, quartered if large (13 ounces)

4 sprigs fresh thyme

1 tablespoon olive oil

½ teaspoon sugar

½ teaspoon salt

Freshly ground pepper to taste

makes 1½ cups

Preheat the oven to 275°. Line a sheet tray with parchment paper or a silicone baking mat. In a bowl, combine the strawberries, tomatoes, thyme, olive oil, sugar, salt and pepper and toss gently to coat.

Spread the fruit in an even layer on the sheet tray and bake for 1 hour and 30 minutes to 1 hour and 45 minutes without stirring or turning. (The roasting time will vary depending on the moisture content, so watch the fruit carefully to make sure nothing burns.) The strawberries and tomatoes should be shriveled but still a bit juicy.

When the fruit is done, transfer it from the sheet tray to a bowl. Serve immediately or cover and refrigerate for up to 1 week.

Strawberry, Tomato & Avocado Salsa

Almost anywhere tomatoes go, strawberries can go, too. Salsa serves as a good home for them, where their juicy, bright flavor mixes well with chiles, lime, avocado and cilantro. This recipe makes enough for a party, but it can easily be halved. The salsa also makes a refreshing accompaniment for fish tacos and grilled shrimp or scallops.

4 cups strawberries, hulled and diced into ½-inch pieces (about 1 pound whole)

1 avocado, diced into ½-inch pieces (1½ cups)

1 habanero pepper, seeded and finely diced (2 teaspoons)

1 large beefsteak tomato, diced into ½-inch pieces (2 cups)

1 teaspoon lime zest

2 teaspoons fresh lime juice

2 tablespoons chopped cilantro

½ medium red onion—peeled, finely diced and rinsed 3 times (6 tablespoons)

½ teaspoon salt

1 tablespoon olive oil

Combine all ingredients in a large bowl and gently stir to mix.

Strawberry Tart with Goat Cheese Filling

This tart is an homage to a dessert that was on the menu at The Commissary in Philadelphia, where I worked when I was a teenager. I could—and often did—eat several Strawberry Heart Tarts during my shift, though I never seemed to gain weight. What I loved most about them was the layer of chocolate under the creamy filling, which I've replicated here; it keeps the crust crisp indefinitely. Sweetened goat cheese adds a tangy note to the easy-to-prepare filling.

For the tart shell:

1½ cups all-purpose flour, plus more for rolling

¼ cup plus 2 tablespoons confectioners' sugar

⅛ teaspoon salt

¼ teaspoon baking powder

1 stick (8 tablespoons) cold butter, cut into small pieces

1 large egg, lightly beaten

1 large egg yolk, lightly beaten

For the filling:

5 ounces soft, mild goat cheese

¼ cup plus 2 tablespoons confectioners' sugar

½ teaspoon pure vanilla extract

8 ounces crème fraîche

3 ounces semisweet or bittersweet chocolate, chopped

¼ cup strawberry preserves

4 cups strawberries, hulled and sliced (about 1 pound whole)

Make the tart shell: In a food processor, pulse the flour, confectioners' sugar, salt and baking powder. Add the butter and pulse to combine until the butter is in small pea-size pieces. Combine the whole egg and egg yolk and, with the food processor running, slowly add the egg through the feed tube. Stop the machine just as the dough begins to come together. Transfer the dough to a flour-dusted surface and knead it once or twice to make sure it is well mixed. Wrap the dough in plastic, flatten it into a disk and refrigerate until firm, at least 1 hour.

Make the filling: Preheat the oven to 375°. In a stand mixer with a paddle attachment, blend the goat cheese, confectioners' sugar and vanilla at medium speed until smooth. Add the crème fraîche and gently mix at low speed until just combined (do not mix this in a food processor as it will curdle). Transfer to a bowl and refrigerate until needed.

On a well-floured surface, roll the dough out to form a 12-inch circle. Press the dough into a 10-inch tart pan with a removable bottom and tuck the excess between the dough and the tart pan sides to reinforce the edges. Prick the dough all over with a fork and chill in the refrigerator for 15 minutes or until firm.

Line the tart shell with foil, fill with dry beans or pie weights and bake for 20 to 25 minutes until firm and dry. Remove the foil and continue to bake, uncovered, until golden brown, about 15 minutes more. Cool completely. (You can make the tart shell up to 2 days ahead.)

Melt the chocolate in a microwave oven in 20-second intervals, stirring in between, until it's melted and smooth. Pour the chocolate into the cooled tart shell and smooth with a spatula. Chill in the refrigerator until the chocolate hardens.

In a small saucepan, heat the strawberry preserves and 1 tablespoon of water over medium heat until the preserves liquefy enough to create a glaze. Meanwhile, spread the goat cheese mixture over the layer of chocolate in the tart shell and top with the sliced strawberries. Brush the strawberries with glaze. Serve immediately or refrigerate for several hours before serving.

Strawberry Tarte Tatin

This is an "against all odds" dessert. It defies the French rule that a true tarte Tatin is made with apples. It also defies logic, since strawberries release considerably more juice than apples, which threatens to turn the pastry into a giant, fruity mess. But the combination of strawberries, puff pastry and caramel was too much for me to resist. The gamble paid off: The concentrated flavor of strawberries is a nice contrast to the heady aromatics of butter and vanilla. I cheated and added some flour to thicken the considerable amount of berry juice. It's still on the juicy side, but if you're like me, you won't mind.

- 1 sheet puff pastry, thawed
- ¼ cup all-purpose flour, plus more for rolling
- 1 cup granulated sugar
- ½ stick (4 tablespoons) butter, cut into pieces
- ½ teaspoon fleur de sel or other coarse salt
- ½ teaspoon pure vanilla bean paste (available at specialty food stores or online)
- 4½ cups strawberries, hulled (about 1¼ pounds whole)

serves -4-

Choose four baking dishes, 4 to 5 inches in diameter or about 12 ounces each, and place them on a baking sheet lined with foil or parchment paper. On a well-floured surface, roll the puff pastry into a rectangle about ⅛-inch thick, large enough to cut into 4 circles that are slightly larger than the dishes. Prick the pastry all over with a fork, then transfer the circles to a baking sheet lined with parchment paper and refrigerate.

Preheat the oven to 300°. In a medium pot, stir together the sugar and ¼ cup water and bring the mixture to a boil over medium-high heat. Brush the sides of the pan down with water to dissolve any sugar crystals sticking to the sides of the pan. Reduce the heat to medium and cook, swirling occasionally, until the mixture begins to thicken and turn dark amber, about 7 minutes. Remove from the heat and carefully stir in the butter. Pour into a metal bowl and quickly mix in the fleur de sel and vanilla paste. Immediately divide the caramel among the 4 baking dishes.

In a large bowl, toss the strawberries with the ¼ cup flour. Place as many strawberries as possible, hulled-side down, in a tight layer over the caramel in each dish. Cut the remaining strawberries in half and divide them among the dishes, hulled side facing up. Transfer the baking sheet with the dishes to the oven and bake, uncovered, for 20 minutes.

Remove the baking sheet and let the dishes cool slightly. Meanwhile, increase the oven temperature to 400°. Top each dish with a circle of the puff pastry, tucking any excess into the sides of the dishes. Bake for 20 to 25 minutes, until the strawberry mixture is bubbling and the puff pastry is golden brown. Transfer the dishes to a rack to cool completely. Cool until the liquid has thickened, 2 to 3 hours.

When ready to serve, invert each cooled tart onto a plate. Serve with vanilla ice cream. If you're not serving the tarts right away, then leave them in their dishes until ready to unmold and serve.

Strawberry, Apricot & Almond Tart

The almond-y crust of this free-form tart is tender, and it's no match for the cascade of juices the fruit releases. I considered substituting a sturdier dough, but this one tastes so good that I couldn't bring myself to do it. Keeping that in mind, I find the tart is best made in a 12-inch cast-iron skillet or other shallow metal pan. It can also be made directly on a sheet pan lined with parchment, but the juices are likely to burst forth and they tend to burn on the pan. A copper tarte Tatin pan would also be a great vessel should you be lucky enough to own one.

For the dough:

2 cups all-purpose flour, plus extra for rolling

2 tablespoons sugar

¾ teaspoon coarse salt

1½ sticks (12 tablespoons) cold butter, cut into small pieces

¼ cup sliced almonds, plus more for finishing the tart

¼ cup ice water

For the filling:

¼ cup sliced almonds

3 tablespoons flour

¼ cup plus ⅓ cup sugar, divided, plus more for sprinkling

1 pound strawberries, hulled and halved (quartered if very large), about 3 cups

4 fresh apricots, pitted and sliced

2 tablespoons unsalted butter

serves —8—

Make the dough: Pulse the flour, sugar and salt in a food processor. Add the butter and almonds and pulse to combine until the butter is in small pea-size pieces. With the machine running, quickly add the water and stop the machine just as the dough begins to come together. Transfer the dough to a flour-dusted surface and knead it once or twice to make sure it's well mixed. Wrap the dough in plastic, flatten it into a disk and refrigerate until firm, at least 1 hour.

Preheat the oven to 400°. On a well-floured surface, roll the dough into a rough circle about 14 inches in diameter. Transfer the dough to a 12-inch paella pan or other large, shallow pan. Patch any holes or tears with a bit of cold water and refrigerate until firm, about 15 minutes.

Make the filling: In a mini food processor, pulse the almonds until finely ground. Add the flour and the ¼ cup sugar and pulse to combine well. Spread the mixture evenly in the center of the rolled dough. In a medium bowl, combine the strawberries and apricots. Scatter the fruit on top of the almond mixture and sprinkle with the remaining ⅓ cup of sugar. Dot with the 2 tablespoons of butter.

Fold the edges of the dough inward over the fruit toward the center of the tart, leaving a large opening. Brush the crust with cold water and sprinkle with the reserved sliced almonds and sugar. Transfer the tart to the oven and bake for 45 to 50 minutes or until the filling is bubbling and the tart is golden brown all over. Let cool slightly before serving.

Strawberry Hand Pies

The key to these flat little pies is an extra-flaky crust, which is achieved by keeping the pie dough cold (thus the frozen butter). Retaining that cold temperature every step of the way is essential, so clear out a space in your fridge or freezer where you can easily and repeatedly chill the baking sheets as you work. Whenever the dough starts to feel soft, chill it until it's firm again.

---

2 cups all-purpose flour, plus more for rolling and sprinkling

1 teaspoon granulated sugar

½ teaspoon coarse salt

1¾ sticks (14 tablespoons) frozen butter, cut into small pieces

¼ cup ice water

¼ cup strawberry preserves (or Strawberry Freezer Jam, page 20)

1½ cups sliced strawberries

2 tablespoons raw sugar

makes 10

In a food processor, pulse the flour, sugar and salt. Add the butter and pulse to combine until the mixture forms small pea-size pieces. With the machine running, quickly add the water and stop the machine just as the dough begins to come together. Remove the dough and knead once or twice to make sure it is combined. Divide the dough into 2 equal balls. Wrap each ball in plastic, flatten into disks and refrigerate until firm but not rock hard, 15 to 30 minutes.

On a flour-dusted surface, roll each piece of dough into a rough 10-by-12-inch rectangle, chilling them on parchment-paper-lined baking sheets as you go. Using a fluted pastry wheel, trim each rectangle into a neat 9-by-11-inch rectangle. Knead the scraps together and chill. Cut the first large rectangle into 8 rectangles and space them out on a baking sheet.

Sprinkle ½ teaspoon of flour in the center of each small rectangle and top with about 1 teaspoon of the preserves and 4 or 5 of the strawberry slices. Cut the second large rectangle into 8 smaller rectangles in the same manner as the first, then cut a large S-shaped vent vertically in each one. Brush the perimeter of the strawberry-topped pastry pieces with water and top each one with a piece of dough, pressing down firmly to seal them. Chill the pies until firm.

Preheat the oven to 375°. Roll the reserved scraps out to make 4 more rectangles and repeat the above process to create two additional pies. Place them on another baking sheet. Brush the top of each pie with water, then sprinkle with some of the raw sugar. Transfer the baking sheets to the oven and bake for 30 minutes or until the pies are golden brown on top. Transfer the pies to a cooling rack immediately so they don't stick. Serve as soon as they are cool enough to eat.

Gingered Strawberry-Rhubarb Crisp

Making a fruit crumble is a surefire way to make people weak in the knees with very little effort. Here, ginger makes an appearance in three forms: chopped candied ginger and ground ginger in the topping, plus freshly grated ginger in the fruit mixture. If you don't happen to have all three on hand, the crisp will still be excellent without one of them—but the trifecta really makes this dessert sing.

For the topping:

1 cup plus 2 tablespoons all-purpose flour

⅓ cup light brown sugar

2 tablespoons granulated sugar

¾ teaspoon cinnamon

½ teaspoon ground ginger

¼ teaspoon baking powder

¼ teaspoon coarse salt

1 stick (8 tablespoons) cold butter, cut into pieces

⅓ cup rolled oats

2 tablespoons chopped candied ginger

For the filling:

4 cups strawberries, hulled and halved, quartered if large (about 1 pound whole)

1 pound rhubarb, cut into ½-inch pieces (about 3 cups)

½ cup granulated sugar

3 tablespoons flour

Grated zest of 1 lemon

Make the crumble: In the bowl of a food processor, combine the flour, brown sugar, granulated sugar, cinnamon, ground ginger, baking powder and salt and pulse to combine. Add the butter and pulse until the mixture becomes clumpy and looks moist throughout. Add the oats and candied ginger and pulse a few times to combine. Transfer to a bowl, cover and refrigerate until ready to use.

Make the filling: Preheat the oven to 375°. In a medium bowl, combine the strawberries, rhubarb, sugar, flour and lemon zest.

Spread the fruit out in a 3-quart baking dish and sprinkle with the topping. Bake for 35 to 40 minutes or until the fruit is bubbling all over and the topping is golden brown. Let cool slightly before serving.

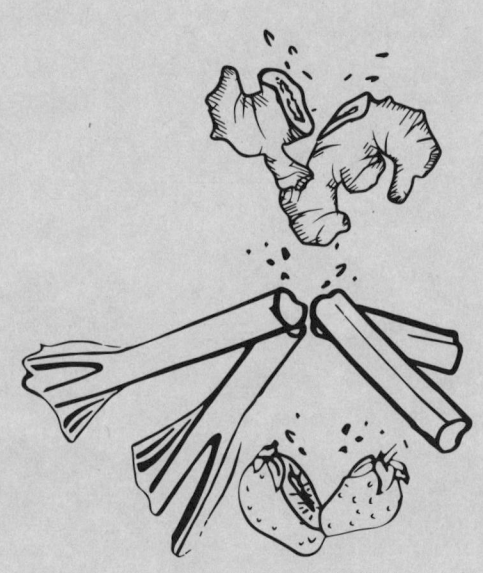

Ice Pops with Hazelnut Chocolate

I'm of the opinion that chocolate improves almost anything. These simple ice pops are redolent with fresh strawberry flavor and studded with little bits of chocolate with hazelnuts. If you don't have ice pop molds, use small paper cups and peel the paper off just before serving.

6 cups strawberries, hulled (about 1½ pounds whole)

2 tablespoons sugar, plus more to taste

One 3-ounce bar dark chocolate with hazelnuts, finely chopped

Special Equipment:

Ten 3-ounce ice pop molds and wooden popsicle sticks

Puree the strawberries, sugar and ½ cup water in a blender until very smooth.

Divide the strawberry mixture among the ice pop molds, leaving about ½-inch of space at the top. Reserve and chill any remaining strawberry mixture; freeze the ice pops for 1 hour or until the mixture has started to thicken.

Divide the chopped chocolate among the ice pop molds and stir each with an ice pop stick to evenly disperse the chocolate throughout the strawberry mixture. Top off with the reserved strawberry mixture if necessary. Insert the sticks in the molds and freeze for at least 3 more hours or up to overnight. Dip the molds in hot water briefly to release the ice pops and serve immediately.

Roasted Strawberry-Basil Frozen Yogurt

I love marrying the flavor of basil with strawberries. The herb adds a complexity that's hard to identify and easy to like. Enhanced by the vanilla in this recipe, the combination has an intoxicating perfume all its own. After spending a few hours in the freezer, the yogurt has the ideal texture, but if you're storing it for longer, you can easily revive it from its rock-hard state with a few blasts in the microwave.

4½ cups strawberries, hulled (about 1¼ pounds whole)

1¼ cups sugar

½ vanilla bean, split and scraped

4 to 6 fresh basil leaves

2 cups nonfat Greek yogurt

Pinch of salt

Preheat the oven to 425°. In a medium glass or ceramic baking dish, stir together the strawberries, sugar and vanilla-bean pod and seeds. Transfer to the oven and roast for 5 minutes, then stir and roast for another 5 minutes.

Discard the vanilla pod and transfer the contents of the baking dish to the jar of a blender. Add the basil leaves and let stand for 5 minutes, then blend until smooth. Cool completely.

In a large bowl, whisk together the strawberry puree, yogurt and salt. Freeze the mixture in an ice cream maker according to manufacturer's instructions. Transfer to an airtight container and chill in the freezer for 1 to 2 hours for a soft texture. Or freeze until needed, then soften at room temperature or with short bursts in the microwave until the yogurt is soft enough to scoop. The yogurt will keep for several weeks in an airtight container in the freezer.

Lemony Cornmeal Strawberry Shortcakes

There are lots of different ideas about the definition of strawberry shortcake. For some people, it's sponge cake layered with whipped cream and strawberries, but for me, it always involves a biscuit. The key to good strawberry shortcake is capturing the freshness of all the elements by combining them just before serving. The shortcakes should be a bit warm, the cream freshly whipped and the strawberries macerated just long enough to coax out their ruby red juice. I love the grittiness that cornmeal gives these lemon-tinged biscuits; it adds another dimension to the classic. No book on strawberries would be complete without a shortcake recipe!

For the shortcakes:

2 cups all-purpose flour, plus more for kneading

½ cup finely ground yellow cornmeal

1 tablespoon baking powder

¾ teaspoon salt

¼ cup granulated sugar

Finely grated zest of 1 lemon (1 tablespoon)

¾ stick (6 tablespoons) cold butter, cut into pieces

1¼ cup heavy cream, plus more for brushing

1 tablespoon raw sugar

For the strawberries:

2½ cups strawberries, hulled and quartered (about 12 ounces whole)

½ cup granulated sugar

2 tablespoons fresh lemon juice

For the lemon cream:

3 tablespoons homemade or jarred lemon curd

1 cup heavy cream

serves 8

Preheat the oven to 400°. Line a baking sheet with parchment paper.

Make the shortcakes: In a food processor, pulse the flour, cornmeal, baking powder, salt, sugar and lemon zest. Add the butter and pulse to combine until the mixture forms small pea-size pieces.

Add the 1¼ cups of heavy cream and pulse until the dough just begins to come together. Transfer the dough to a lightly floured surface and knead once or twice to make sure it is well mixed. Pat the dough into a 10-inch-by-5-inch rectangle a little less than 1 inch thick. Cut the dough into 8 equal square pieces and transfer them to the prepared baking sheet. Brush the tops of the shortcakes with cream and sprinkle with some of the raw sugar. Bake until golden brown on top and cooked through, about 25 to 30 minutes. Place on a rack to cool.

Meanwhile, combine the strawberries, sugar and lemon juice and let the mixture macerate while the shortcakes bake.

In a medium bowl, whisk together the lemon curd and cream. Using a stand or hand mixer, whip the lemon cream at medium-high speed until it is satiny and holds its shape.

Slice the cooled shortcakes in half crosswise. To assemble, place one shortcake half on a plate. Spoon about ¼ cup of the strawberry mixture along with some of the juice onto the shortcake bottom, layer with a dollop of lemon cream and top with the remaining shortcake half. Repeat with the other cakes, strawberries and cream and serve immediately.

Summer Berry Pudding

I can't understand why summer pudding, a beloved British dessert, is virtually unknown in the United States. It has all the hallmarks of an ideal warm-weather dish: It's a cinch to make, very pretty, very tasty and beautifully highlights the season's bounty. Your shopping list is short here: berries, sugar, a lemon and a loaf of white bread. The only variable is how much juice the fruit will release; you may have to hold some of it back to avoid over-saturating the bread.

---

4 cups strawberries, hulled and sliced lengthwise (about 1 pound whole)

One 6-ounce container blueberries (1 heaping cup)

2 tablespoons fresh lemon juice

¼ cup sugar

One 6-ounce container raspberries (about 1 cup)

10 to 12 slices good white bread (sliced ½-inch thick)

Whipped cream, ice cream or sorbet, for serving

serves 6

Line each cup of a standard 6-cup muffin tin with plastic wrap.

Place the strawberries, blueberries, lemon juice and sugar in a medium saucepan and cook over medium-high heat for 5 to 7 minutes or until all the sugar has dissolved and the mixture just begins to bubble. (It should look like fruit soup.) Transfer to a bowl and add the raspberries, tossing gently until combined. Let cool completely.

Use a biscuit cutter, glass or knife to cut 6 slices of bread into rounds that are the same diameter as the bottom of a muffin cup (about

2¼ inches). You may be able to get two rounds out of one piece of bread. Place one round in the bottom of each muffin cup. Cut the remaining 6 slices of bread into slightly larger rounds that are the same diameter as the top of the muffin cups (about 3 inches). Reserve the bread scraps for another use.

Using a spoon, fill each muffin cup nearly to the top with the berry mixture. They should look juicy but not overflowing. (You may have some berries left over; save those for serving the puddings.)

Dip one side of a large bread round in the excess liquid and place it, dipped side up, on top of a muffin cup, pressing down lightly. Repeat with the remaining bread rounds. Fold the overhanging plastic wrap over each pudding and wrap the entire muffin tin in plastic. Lightly press down on the puddings. Refrigerate overnight.

When ready to serve, remove and unwrap each pudding and place on a plate; add whipped cream, ice cream or sorbet, plus any remaining berries spooned over the top, and serve while still cold.

Eton Mess

This dessert was traditionally served at the annual June 4 celebration at England's Eton College (which commemorated the birthday of King George III), but the combination of meringue, whipped cream and strawberries cannot be beat, which explains its enduring popularity. A Pavlova combines the same elements in a more formal presentation, but here the meringues are crumbled and layered in a glass. I've lightened the cream with yogurt to make this an almost-healthy dessert (also because I like the tanginess of the yogurt).

For the meringues:
- 2 large egg whites
- ½ cup granulated sugar
- Pinch cream of tartar
- ½ teaspoon vanilla extract

For the filling:
- 8 cups whole strawberries
- ¼ cup granulated sugar
- Splash of liqueur, such as Kirsch or St-Germain
- 2 cups nonfat Greek Yogurt
- 2 cups heavy cream
- ¼ cup confectioners' sugar
- ½ teaspoon vanilla extract

serves -8-

Make the meringues: Combine the egg whites, the ½ cup of granulated sugar and the cream of tartar in the bowl of an electric mixer set over a pan of simmering water. Whisk constantly until the sugar is completely dissolved and the mixture is hot to the touch, about 3 minutes. Transfer the bowl to a stand mixer fitted with the whisk attachment and beat until stiff, glossy peaks form, 5 to 7 minutes. Mix in the vanilla.

Preheat the oven to 225°. Spread the meringue out to a thickness of about ½ inch on a baking sheet lined with parchment paper. Bake for

2 hours, lowering the heat to 200° if the meringue begins to brown. Turn off the oven and leave the meringue inside until the oven has cooled. Break the meringue into large pieces and store in an airtight container or resealable plastic bag if not using right away. It will keep for several days.

Cut the strawberries into quarters and toss with the ¼ cup of granulated sugar and the liqueur in a large bowl. Let sit at room temperature until juicy, about 30 minutes, tossing occasionally.

In a bowl, whip the yogurt, cream, confectioners' sugar and vanilla together until soft peaks form. Crumble half of the meringue and divide among eight 8-ounce glasses. Top with half of the cream mixture, followed by half of the strawberries. Repeat the layering with the remaining ingredients. Serve immediately or refrigerate and serve withing a few hours.

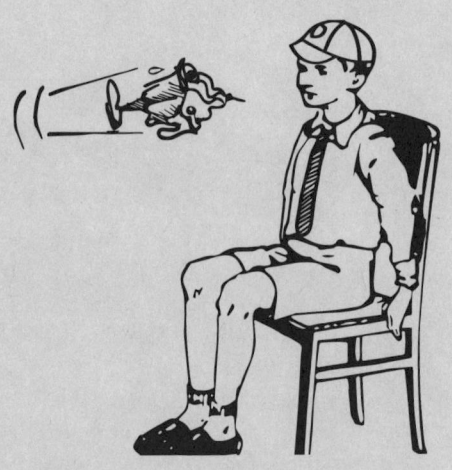

Strawberry Smoothie

On the East Coast, strawberry season is painfully short, so I spend most of it mulling over how to prolong my supply of this favorite fruit. One of the easiest ways is freezing the strawberries. I freeze as many berries as I can, then pull from my stash throughout the summer to make sorbets, sauces and afternoon smoothies. The flavor of local beauties really transforms this smoothie. When I want to make more of a meal of it, I add a handful of almonds. Tip: Unless you own a powerful Vitamix blender, microwave the berries for 10 to 15 seconds to soften them before pureeing.

---

3 cups frozen strawberries (see Note)

2 medium bananas, broken into chunks

1½ cups liquid yogurt or kefir

½ cup coconut water

Dash of pure vanilla extract

1 teaspoon raw sugar

serves 2

Combine all the ingredients in a blender and blend until smooth. Divide into two glasses and serve.

Note: To freeze strawberries, wash, hull and halve them, then place them on a baking sheet lined with paper towels to remove excess moisture. When the berries are completely dry, remove the paper towels and place the baking sheet in the freezer uncovered. Every 20 minutes or so, give the berries a stir with your hands to loosen them from the baking sheet and each other until they are frozen hard, about 1 hour. Transfer the berries to a resealable plastic bag and freeze for up to 6 weeks.

Pink Sangria

Sangria is always a good choice for summer entertaining, though I prefer a lighter, whiter version to the traditional red wine, brandy and apple concoction. This one, made with dry rosé, St-Germain and Aperol (a bitter rhubarb-flavored aperitif), is far from traditional, but it's so refreshing on a summer's evening and easy to make for a crowd; just double or triple the recipe if you need to.

3½ cups strawberries, hulled (about 1 pound whole)
2 limes, sliced into ⅛-inch wheels
1 bottle of dry rosé, chilled
6 ounces St-Germain elderflower liqueur
2 ounces Aperol
Sparkling water, for serving

serves 8

Slice about two-thirds of the berries until you have 2 cups, then transfer to a serving pitcher. Puree the remaining berries in a food processor or blender and add them to the pitcher along with the lime slices. Add the wine, St-Germain and Aperol to the pitcher and stir. Chill for at least an hour before serving. Fill glasses with ice, then add sangria and some of the fruit, top with sparkling water, stir and serve.

Thank You!

Short Stack gives its endless gratitude to those who inspired us to create a new kind of food publication, and its deepest thanks to those who helped us see it through: Julia and Paul Child, Ashley Christensen, Charman Driver, William Hereford, Jordan McIntyre, Mom, Alyssa Pagano, Bonnie Slotnick, Abby Tannenbaum, Frank Thompson, Tina Ujlaki, Will Schwalbe and the folks at the YAI Network.

The author would like to thank Rhoda Boone, Afton Hall, Pearl Jones and Steven Kasher, as well as Jim and Jennifer Pike for their wonderful strawberries year after year and all of the strawberry growers at the Union Square Greenmarket.

You wouldn't be holding this book without the generosity and enthusiasm of our 1,761 Kickstarter backers, including those who gave a little extra to be named here: Scott Hocker, Victoria Hunton, Juliana Minium, Kitty Morgan, Shannen Naegel, Robert Rembert, Carrie Ross, Heidi Swanson, Brandy Valdez and Cliff Wu.

Share your Short Stack cooking experiences with us (or just keep in touch) via:

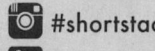 #shortstackeds 📘 facebook.com/shortstackeditions
@shortstackeds ✉ hello@shortstackeditions.com

Colophon

This edition of Short Stack was printed by Stephen Gould Corp. in Richmond, Virginia on Mohawk Britehue Meadow Green (interior) and Neenah Oxford White (cover) paper. The main text of the book is set in Futura and Jensen Pro, and the headlines are set in Lobster.

Available now at ShortStackEditions.com:

Vol. 1 | Eggs,
by Ian Knauer

Vol. 2 | Tomatoes,
by Soa Davies

Vol. 3 | Strawberries,
by Susan Spungen

Vol. 4 | Buttermilk,
by Angie Mosier

Vol. 5 | Grits,
by Virginia Willis

Vol. 6 | Sweet Potatoes,
by Scott Hocker

Vol. 7 | Broccoli,
by Tyler Kord

Vol. 8 | Honey,
by Rebekah Peppler

Vol. 9 | Plums,
by Martha Holmberg

Vol. 10 | Corn,
by Jessica Battilana

Vol. 11 | Apples,
by Andrea Albin

Vol. 12 | Brown Sugar,
by Libbie Summers

Vol. 13 | Lemons,
by Alison Roman

Vol. 14 | Prosciutto di Parma,
by Sara Jenkins

Vol. 15 | Summer Squash,
by Sarah Baird

Vol. 16 | Peaches,
by Beth Lipton

Vol. 17 | Chickpeas,
by Victoria Granof

Vol. 18 | Chocolate,
by Susie Heller

Vol. 19 | Maple Syrup,
by Casey Elsass

Vol. 20 | Rhubarb,
by Sheri Castle

Vol. 21 | Cherries,
by Stacy Adimando

Vol. 22 | Eggplant,
by Raquel Pelzel

Vol. 23 | Tahini,
by Adeena Sussman

Vol. 24 | Ginger,
by Mindy Fox

Vol. 25 | Avocados,
by Katie Quinn

Vol. 26 | Peanuts,
by Steven Satterfield

Vol. 27 | Coconut,
by Ben Mims

Vol. 28 | Cucumbers,
by Dawn Perry

Vol. 29 | Pears,
by Andrea Slonecker